Nobody Told Me This About Raising a Bilingual Child

A Beginner's Guide to Bilingual Parenting

Janny Perez

Nobody Told Me This About Raising a Bilingual Child

Copyright © 2023 by Janny Perez

The information conveyed by Janny Perez in this book, including, without limitation, any information contained in this book, is intended to provide you with basic instruction regarding raising a bilingual child. The content is for educational purposes only. Neither Mi Legasi LLC nor Janny Perez in this course (book) guarantee nor predict any results or return on investment based on the information you receive in this course or this workbook. Mi Legasi LLC suggests you consult with an independent professional or consultant before embarking on any specifics regarding your child, as every child is different.

Printed in the United States of America
Cover Designer: Janny Perez

Paperback ISBN: 979-8-9880488-0-0
Hardcover ISBN: 979-8-9880488-1-7

The Publishing Pad
www.thepublishingpad.com

Para mi 'apá en el cielo, quien me enseño
cuan valioso es pasar la cultura y lenguaje a
nuestros hijos para un mejor futuro.
Gracias 'apa.

For my dad in heaven, who taught me
how valuable it is to pass on culture and language to
our children for a better future.
Thanks dad.

Table of
CONTENTS

Babies Start Learning in The Womb.................................... 11

Your Spouse May Not Care Much About Raising a Bilingual Child... 14

What the Heck MLAH or OPOL was until I Googled it..................... 21

They Will Tell You, "This Method is The Best Method."................... 26

What a Language Plan Is and Why You Need One........................... 28

The REAL Costs Involved in Raising a Bilingual Child...................... 32

What the Language "Golden Years" are and Why it Matters...or Not... 36

Why Need and Exposure Matter.. 40

Importance of Creating a Positive Emotional Connection to the Language for My Child... 43

Consistently Speaking Spanish (or the minority language) May Be Hard.. 48

Trust Your Instincts Even if It Goes Against the Experts.................. 51

It Will Be a Roller Coaster Ride.. 55

As the Child Gets Older, it Will Be Easier And Yet More Challenging 58

Having a Language Network is Imperative................................. 62

You Will Want to Give up Many Times..................................... 66

It is Very Lonely at Times and You'll Learn to Be "Unpopular".. 70

This is Actually an Amazing Gift With More Benefits Than You Realize.. 74

Some Helpful Resources.. 81

Become an Online Student and Learn How To Raise a Bilingual Spanish Child Your Way.. 82

Hola, Hola. I'm Janny Perez

Welcome

I know you want to get straight to the good stuff, so I'll make sure to keep it short and highlight what you may be interested in learning.

- I am not a language specialist or speech pathologist — however, I have interviewed many of them on my podcast along with dozens of parents raising bilingual Spanish kids.
- I am not a Spanish teacher, but I have been a college teacher and mentor and am now a bilingual parenting motivator and educator.
- I am a bilingual Latina mom, raising a multilingual (English, Spanish, Bulgarian) & multicultural child.

How Can I Help *You?*

I wrote this book with you in mind to give you an honest perspective on raising a bilingual child. One that perhaps you won't get from traditional bilingual parenting books. You see, when I started raising my daughter bilingually, I really didn't know how I was going to do it. I tried to educate myself as much as I could, but honestly, Nobody Told Me This About Bilingual Parenting...so I want to tell you.

Janny Perez

Who is This Book For?

While anybody can most certainly read this book, I think the ones that would benefit the most from it are:

- Families that are expecting or have babies and want to raise bilingual children but don't know where or how to start.

- Families with children 0-6 years old that would like to raise bilingual children but may think it's too late.

- For people with limited time that want practical tools and tips on raising bilingual children.

- Speech and language pathologists or language specialists that want to give parents tips and tools to use with their kids.

- Friends or family members that want to give a unique baby shower gift to the parent-to-be.

- People that may feel alone in this bilingual parenting journey and want to feel heard.

- Language teachers or schools that want to support their student's language learning by supporting parents with this tool.

you

How to Use This Book

This book was purposely designed to be an easy read. I find that most bilingual parenting books get very technical into the science of bilingualism and the brain. They don't necessarily focus on practical tips or exercises that help the parent. What ends up happening is that you get overwhelmed with it all and see it as something perhaps unachievable.

My goal is not to overwhelm you but to provide you with my honest experience, and give you practical tips and exercises that will actually help you in this bilingual parenting journey. I encourage you to sit and take the time to do the exercises.

Something very powerful happens when you bring a pen to paper. It's like telling your brain, "this matters," and your brain will likely make it a priority in your life. If you are not sure of an answer, you can skip it as you learn more and then go back to it.

I am so happy and honored you decided to pick up this book. You're on your way to getting that boost of confidence or reassurance that YOU CAN raise a bilingual child.

I know you can!

You may not realize that another language is one of the best gifts you can ever give your child. Language is the door to culture, emotions, memories, thoughts, opportunities, and your legacy.

—Janny Perez

Nobody told me...

Babies Start Learning in the Womb

When I was pregnant with my daughter, I knew I wanted to raise her bilingually, but I figured that was something that would happen "eventually." I had no idea I could've and should've started speaking to her in Spanish while I was still pregnant. It was only until my daughter was out of the womb, walking, and you might say, already in school, that I found out that babies start language development in the womb! That's right.

According to numerous research studies, babies as early as 25 weeks can start to recognize speech patterns.

Dr. Liz Donner at Baby Center reviewed the following:

"Between 16 and 22 weeks of pregnancy, your baby may start to hear faint sounds inside your body such as the noise made by your breathing, heartbeat, and digestion.

After 23 weeks, your baby can hear sounds from the outside world, including your voice.

Researchers have found that babies in the womb learn to recognize their mother's voice and prefer it to other voices.

At around 26 weeks, your baby may begin to respond to the sounds they hear with changes in their heartbeat, breathing, and movement."

So if you begin practicing and speaking Spanish or any minority language while pregnant, your baby will be born accustomed to the nuanced sounds of the minority language.

Forget about playing classical music to your baby, just kidding, and don't tell my musician husband I said that, but seriously, use this opportunity to speak to your baby in Español or whatever minority language you want them to speak.

Boy, I wish somebody would've told me that!

Language Activities for Parents

To Encourage Language Development in Babies

Sing to Baby in the Minority Language

Practice Narrating in the Minority Language

Speak to Baby in the Minority Language

Read to Baby in the Minority Language

Speak to Friends & Family in the Minority Language

Listen to Music in the Minority Language

"Vamos a leer un libro..."

Nobody told me...

Your Spouse May Not Care Much About Raising a Bilingual Child

Another shocker!

When I was pregnant with my daughter, I figured WE'D raise her bilingually. I assumed that I would speak Spanish, my husband would speak Bulgarian to her, and she'd learn English at some point.

Well, none of that happened because, much to my surprise, my husband barely spoke to her in Bulgarian once our baby was born. Two things happened: 1) He was much more comfortable speaking English to her, and 2) English was our everyday language.

He also didn't show as much interest in "teaching" her Bulgarian. The fact that I was adamant that I wanted her to be exposed to 3 languages didn't click with my husband until our daughter started Kindergarten. Now, my husband is much more interested and involved in our daughter's language learning, but in the beginning, I can tell you, he didn't care much.

Don't assume your spouse or partner is on board with your bilingual parenting.

Please don't assume that they will be involved, perhaps to the same degree that you are or want to be.

Do make sure you have a language conversation or "the language talk," preferably before the child is born, so there aren't surprises or, worst yet, arguments.

I wish somebody would've told me that!

How to Get Your Spouse's Support in Bilingual Parenting

1 Understand their reasoning

Understand their reasons for not wanting to raise a bilingual child and their challenges or fears. Their answers may surprise you.

2 Make them see what's in it for THEM

There are many benefits that come from raising a bilingual child, like enhancing your own cognitive abilities, improving communication with your child, and strengthening family bonds. Show them how THEY can benefit from raising a bilingual.

3 Explain the MANY benefits

There are many benefits to raising a bilingual child. If you need help convincing them, check out my Benefits of Bilingualism page.

4 Discuss YOUR personal reasons

Share with your spouse why it's important for you to raise a bilingual child. Make sure to go beyond the surface and speak from the heart.

5 Set realistic expectations by starting small

Start with small activities like reading a book in the minority language a few times a week before you expect your spouse to be speaking to your child 24/7 in the minority language. Little by little goes a long way.

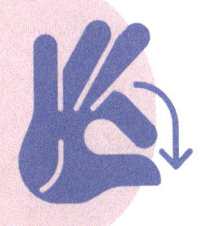

6 Try to understand and not place blame

You cannot force someone to change or do something they don't want to. Instead, try to find a solution and seek outside support. The more you continue to show interest, sooner or later, they'll take notice.

Understanding Your Language Proficiency Exercise

The following page contains a language proficiency and comfort questionnaire for you to complete.

It is important you understand where you are starting from in your bilingual parenting journey. Knowing your starting point means understanding your language proficiency and your comfort level when it comes to the minority language.

If you have a spouse, partner, or someone who will be living with your child, it is good to also gauge their language proficiency and comfort level.

A lower comfort level in any particular area means you may have to supplement this area with additional language exposure or resources. For example, you may feel that you read "very well" in the minority language, but you only speak "moderately well." Therefore, for you to feel more comfortable speaking "very well," you may have to practice speaking in the minority language more than you are now.

Mark the following questions to get a better understanding of your current language proficiency and comfort level.

18

Language Proficiency Questions

I SPEAK THE MINORITY LANGUAGE

- ◯ Very Well
- ◯ Moderately Well
- ◯ Not Well
- ◯ Not At All

MY SPOUSE/PARTNER SPEAKS THE MINORITY LANGUAGE

- ◯ Very Well
- ◯ Moderately Well
- ◯ Not Well
- ◯ Not At All

I READ IN THE MINORITY LANGUAGE

- ◯ Very Well
- ◯ Moderately Well
- ◯ Not Well
- ◯ Not At All

MY SPOUSE/PARTNER READS IN THE MINORITY LANGUAGE

- ◯ Very Well
- ◯ Moderately Well
- ◯ Not Well
- ◯ Not At All

I WRITE IN THE MINORITY LANGUAGE

- ◯ Very Well
- ◯ Moderately Well
- ◯ Not Well
- ◯ Not At All

MY SPOUSE/PARTNER WRITES IN THE MINORITY LANGUAGE

- ◯ Very Well
- ◯ Moderately Well
- ◯ Not Well
- ◯ Not At All

I FEEL COMFORTABLE SPEAKING TO MY CHILD IN THE MINORITY LANGUAGE

- ◯ All of The Time
- ◯ Most of The Time
- ◯ Some of the Time
- ◯ Not At All

MY SPOUSE/PARTNER FEELS COMFORTABLE SPEAKING TO OUR CHILD IN THE MINORITY LANGUAGE

- ◯ All of The Time
- ◯ Most of The Time
- ◯ Some of the Time
- ◯ Not At All

"Bilingual parenting isn't a journey without hiccups. The important thing is to keep offering the home language as often as you can, without feeling guilty if you slip into the dominant tongue. Offer kids this treasure with love and laughter, and through cultural connections, so there is always a positive feeling surrounding bilingualism. "

–Alexandra Alessandri
Bilingual Parenting Mom.
Award Winning Bilingual Children's Book Author

Nobody told me...

What the Heck MLAH or OPOL Was Until I Googled It

"Are you using MLAH or OPOL approach?" It was like asking me what R2D2 and C3PO stand for. I had no clue, and honestly, I still don't know what those robot names in Star Wars stand for!

You must understand that the minute you decide to raise a bilingual child, you become a part of this community that you may or may not know exists.

You will read or come across words like MLAH, OPOL, mother language, minority language, and heritage language, and it can become overwhelming trying to figure it all out.

Lucky for you, I have a cheat sheet so you don't feel like me when my husband starts talking Star Wars and I give him the deer in the headlights look...

Or answer, ¿Qué, qué? What?

OPOL - One Person, One Language Approach

In this approach, one parent speaks with the child in the minority language all the time.
For example, if Mom speaks Spanish and Dad speaks Italian, then Mom will speak and address the child only in Spanish, and Dad will speak to the child only in Italian.

Many people find this approach very successful.
If you prefer this method, the sooner you start, the better, so your child grows up knowing and understanding that one parent = one language and the other = another language.

Hablo Español Solo Con Mami

MLAH - Minority Language at Home Approach

In this approach, both parents speak the minority language at home all the time. For example, if both Mom and Dad speak Spanish, they will speak and communicate with their child only in Spanish. Outside the home, they can choose to speak English or the community language according to the environment or continue speaking Spanish.

En mi hogar Solo se habla Español!

This is a practical approach, as the child is surrounded by the minority language. A parental concern occurs when the child begins school and is perhaps behind his peers with the majority language.

Context, Time, and Space Approach

The context or time and space method requires using each language in a different context or situation, depending on who you are with or where you are. For example, if a child has family members that only speak Spanish, he switches to Spanish so that all the family members can communicate and understand each other.

Another example can be if the child has a nanny that only speaks Spanish. When they are around their nanny, they only have to speak Spanish.

Another example is speaking to your child in the minority language during certain activities like bath time, reading at night, or when the family is together.

This method can also be combined with others.

The more consistent you are with this, the more the child will be able to associate certain people, activities, days, or times with the minority language.

Other Methods...

Other methods for raising bilingual children include dual immersion programs, living abroad, language schools, and others I may need to learn about.

Whatever method you choose, know that you don't have to stick with it. You can try different methods and see what works best for your family.

I was raised bilingually with the MLAH method; remember that one? Just checking. However, we are raising our multilingual daughter with various methods, including a loose OPOL method, context, time, and space approach (Spanish is spoken under specific circumstances or events), and enrolling in a language school. In the future, we are thinking of living abroad.

You don't have to raise your bilingual child precisely like others, but if they ask, you'll know what MLAH, OPOL, or Context, Time, and Space means.

I wish somebody would've told me that!

Language Terminology Cheat Sheet

Native Language 	A person's first language acquired from birth by being in an environment where the language is spoken.
Minority Language	A language spoken by a relatively small number of people in a country or area.
Majority (Community) Language 	The most commonly used native language in a country or area. Note that in some communities, the majority language is sometimes the minority language. Ex: Hispanic communities.
MLAH **Minority Language at Home**	When the minority language is spoken at home all the time by all members.
OPOL **One Person One Language**	When one person or parent speaks only the minority language to the child.
Context, Time, & Space 	When language is spoken with particular people, situations, activities, or periods of time.

Nobody told me...

Everyone Will Tell You, "This Method Is The Best Method."

Now that you're familiar with some of the methods used in raising a bilingual child, don't be surprised if you hear people say that "this method is the best method" for bilingual parenting.

Listen, I totally get it, and I understand that many people, like myself, are either raising bilingually or have successfully raised bilingual children. Many language experts and Spanish teachers are effective and very good at what they do.

After interviewing dozens of moms, language experts, and Spanish teachers, I can tell you that **the best method to raise a bilingual child is using the method/s that works for you and your family.**

Every family is different, every child is different, and every family make is different. There is no cookie-cutter approach to bilingual parenting because of this. This is also why you shouldn't compare your family or child to anyone else's, not "Fulanita or Peranito."

When you understand where you are, where you want to go, and why you want to go there, and have the tools and strategies to get YOUR FAMILY there, **you can successfully raise a bilingual child!**

But your family's journey will not look like any other. That's why when people say to you, "this method is the best method," take it with a grain of salt because unless you try it and are successful at it, you can't know.

You can use one or many methods to raise a bilingual child; they work, and that's not the question. You want to ask yourself, "Which method or methods can work for MY family in particular?"

You may be asking, well, "how would I know?" You know by trying, sticking with a method or strategy, seeing if you get results, but more importantly, seeing if it works with your family's lifestyle.

You're more likely to be consistent and committed to your bilingual parenting journey when it doesn't feel forced, and everyone can tune in to what works for each family member.

I wish somebody would've told me that!

Nobody told me...

What a Language Plan Is and Why You Need One

If you Google "language planning," you will get a definition like "(also known as language engineering) is a deliberate effort to influence the function, structure or acquisition of languages or language varieties within a speech community." Um, ok What?

To make things easy for you, a language plan is basically an outline of the method/s you will use to raise a bilingual child OR a thought-out conversation about how you will raise a bilingual child.

So whether you plan on using the MLAH or the OPOL method or perhaps the Context, Time, and Space Method, having a language plan will help you stay committed to this journey. That's the most important reason because you'll likely want to give up at some point, but I'll talk about that later.

The next time someone asks you, "How are you raising your child bilingually?, your response could be something like, "We are using the MLAH approach along with the Context, Time, and Space. It's what's working for our family."

I wish somebody would've told me that!

My Family's Language Plan

Language Planning Exercise

The following page contains a language planning exercise for you to complete.

Just as important as it is knowing where your starting point is in this bilingual parenting journey, so is understanding where you want to go and what that will look like for your family. That means creating a plan of how you will expose your child to the minority language.

I know it may be difficult for you to envision your life 3, 5, or 10 years from now, especially if you have a baby. However, creating a vision for language will help you plan and pivot along the way.

So think about your language expectations for your child. Do you want them to have a basic understanding of the language, the ability to communicate, or do you want them to be fluent and be able to read, speak, and write?

Once you decide on your expectations, decide what methods you'll be using. Again, this may change along the way but having a plan will get you closer to success!

Mark the following questions to start planning your bilingual parenting journey. You can always come back to it if you're feeling stuck or unsure.

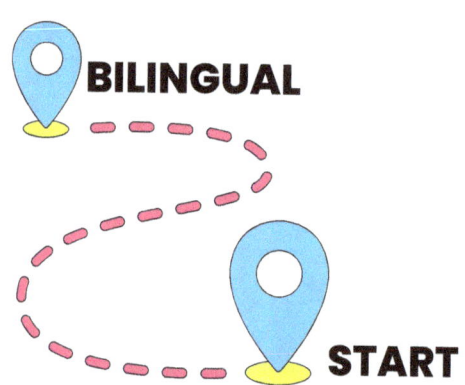

My Family's Language Plan

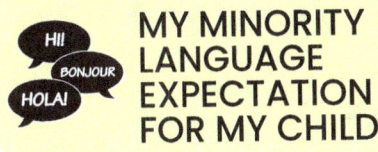 **MY MINORITY LANGUAGE EXPECTATION FOR MY CHILD**

- ◯ Basic Level of Spanish or (ML)
- ◯ Intermediate Level (Can Communicate)
- ◯ Fluency (speak, read, write)

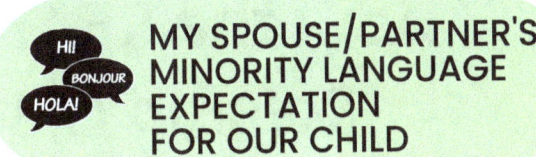 **MY SPOUSE/PARTNER'S MINORITY LANGUAGE EXPECTATION FOR OUR CHILD**

- ◯ Basic Level of Spanish or (ML)
- ◯ Intermediate Level (Can Communicate)
- ◯ Fluency (speak, read, write)

My FAMILY WILL ADOPT THE FOLLOWING LANGUAGE METHOD/S TO RAISE A BILINGUAL CHILD/DREN

- ◯ MLAH – Minority Language at Home
- ◯ OPOL – One Person One Language
- ◯ Context, Time, & Space
- ◯ Other

- ◯ Immersion School
- ◯ Dual Immersion School
- ◯ Online Classes/Online Tutor
- ◯ Living Abroad

I WILL BE SPEAKING TO MY CHILD IN THE MINORITY LANGUAGE

- ◯ All of The Time
- ◯ Most of The Time
- ◯ Some of the Time
- ◯ Not At All

MY SPOUSE/PARTNER WILL BE SPEAKING TO OUR CHILD IN THE MINORITY LANGUAGE

- ◯ All of The Time
- ◯ Most of The Time
- ◯ Some of the Time
- ◯ Not At All

I understand that this may change as my child continues to grow but I am committed to helping my child develop knowledge of a second or even third language.

Signature:_____

Date:_____

Signature: _____

Date: _____

31

Nobody told me...

About the REAL Costs Involved in Raising a Bilingual Child.

Because I grew up surrounded by Spanish, the minority language in our home, I never experienced my parents spending money on classes, tutors, or Spanish education books.

I mean, since we only spoke Spanish at home, it was simply part of our family's lifestyle, so the newspapers, television, and even the activities we did or played were all in Spanish. I got used to waiting for my Spanish comics or a "sopa de letras" word search, a treat from my dad on weekends when he went to a Spanish bookstore.

So fast forward to when I had my daughter, I didn't expect to be spending much on language education, because, well I'm bilingual right? Boy was I wrong.

You see, the less exposure your child gets to the minority language from you, the more outside exposure they will need (If you want them to be a fluent bilingual). This means that you may have to dig deeper into your pockets for them to get the added exposure, and that may mean hiring a minority language nanny, tutors, language schools, etc.

You will experience direct expenses and indirect expenses when it comes to raising a bilingual child.

Direct expenses are clear and have a clear cost. Sometimes, they are a one-time thing, other times, they are recurring, but they are directly linked to the child's bilingual learning. Examples of direct expenses includes books, toys, classes, tutors, subscriptions, etc.

Indirect expenses are not as black and white as direct expenses. These are costs that you may not even think about, but that are linked to your child's language-learning journey. They include the added wear and tear of your car due to the additional miles added from driving your child to language school, potentially lost working hours due to you being more present at home for your child, or having to purchase additional items like a computer or desk so your child has a dedicated space when they take their Spanish or minority language classes.

I wish somebody would've told me that!

Language Budgeting Exercise

The following page contains a language budgeting exercise for you to complete.

1) On the income field, write down how much money comes into the household.

2) Decide what your total weekly budget for language spending will be.

3) Plan out how you will distribute the money.

Having a clear understanding of what you have to work with will help you prepare, so you don't have any unexpected surprises later on.

QUICK TIPS

Create a Language Learning Wishlist for Your Child on Amazon. Keep the list current by adding to it monthly. When a friend or family member wants to buy your child a gift, share this wishlist with them!

Our Family's Language Learning Budget

Description	Week 1	Week 2	Week 3	Week 4	Week 5	Total
Income 1						
Income 2						
Total Budget for Language Learning						
Books, Workbooks, Written Material						
Parenting Resources						
Toys						
Music						
Media & Apps						
Cultural Foods or Items						
Tutors & Classes						
Language Camps						
Travel						

Nobody told me...

What the Language "Golden Years" Are and Why It Matters...or Not.

While anyone can learn a new language at any point in their life, language experts agree that the best time to acquire a new language at a native level is during childhood.

The Golden Years reference the ages between 0 and 6/7 (although more recent studies suggest a child as late as 10) when language learning is at its prime.

According to the Scientific American, "There are three main ideas as to why language-learning ability declines at 18: social changes, interference from one's primary language, and continuing brain development."

By the age of 18, children graduate from school and may not have the time for a second language. Also, how the brain learns changes, making learning more challenging.

So, bottom line. If you want your child to learn a second or third language, start them young and take advantage of their brains!

I wish somebody would've told me that!

" In my 20+ years as an early childhood educator, my experience with bilingual children is that some take longer to speak and therefore cause concern for parents. Regardless if they take longer, I encourage these families to continue speaking to their children in the minority language at home because the child will absorb it. Once the child does begin to speak they tend to be eager and bright learners. The key for parents is to not give up too early."

- Dasy Perez
Expert Early Childhood Educator

Language Development Milestones for Bilingual Babies & Toddlers

0-6 Months

Babies may respond to sounds and voices, and begin to babble.

6-12 Months

Babies start to say their first words, such as "mama" and "dada," and may also start to use simple gestures.

12-18 Months

Toddlers can typically say between 10-50 words in one language and may start to use two-word phrases. They may also begin to understand simple commands and questions.

18-24 Months

Toddlers can say between 50-200 words in one language and may start to use more complex sentences. They may also begin to use both languages and differentiate between them.

Language Development Milestones for Bilingual Children

2-3 Years

Children can typically use complete sentences in both languages, have a vocabulary of 300-1,000 words, and may use basic grammar rules.

3-4 Years

Children can use more complex grammar and have a vocabulary of 1,000-2,000 words in both languages.

4-5 Years
Children may start to read and write in both languages and can have a vocabulary of 2,000-2,500 words in each language.

It's important to note that every child's language development journey is unique, and there is a wide range of what is considered normal. Additionally, bilingual children may have some language skills that are more advanced in one language than the other, which is completely normal. When in doubt, consult a professional.

Why Need and Exposure Matter.

Do you know why I learned Spanish at a native level? It was because I was exposed to the language in a large amount, and I needed to use it if I wanted to communicate with my parents. If I had to put a percentage to it, I'd say it was about 75% -80% in Spanish and the rest was in English from the neighborhood kids. Once we started school, that percentage became more like 50/50.

Research suggests that children need to be exposed to a language for approximately 30% of their waking hours to become fluent in that language. So, for example, if a child is awake for 12 hours a day, then they will need about 25 hours of language exposure a week or about 3.5 hours a day. This exposure can come from various sources, such as parents, siblings, teachers, peers, and media.

Every child is different of course; some children may be ok with less exposure while others may need more. How proficient you want your child to be in the minority language also plays a role.

So for example, if you're ok with your child having general knowledge of the minority language, then a couple of hours a day may be enough. However, if you expect fluency but your child is not getting enough exposure, then some changes need to occur.

30%

When a child has a need to use a language, it helps them become fluent because language proficiency is primarily developed through active communication and practice. It's why children pick up the language so much quicker when they are immersed in it. Have you ever taken your child to your heritage or native country and noticed a difference? Did they pick up a few words or even phrases while they were there?

When children use a language, they are exposed to the nuances of the language, and they learn how to produce and comprehend the language accurately. It's the different words or phrases that you can't translate, like In Spanish, it's words like "trasnochar" (staying up all night, "madrugar" (getting up early), or "estrenar" (showing off something new).

Language acquisition involves both passive and active processes. Children can passively absorb languages by listening to others speak, but active communication is crucial for the development of language skills such as grammar, vocabulary, and pronunciation.

The more the child uses the language, the more confident and motivated they will become to continue learning. When children are able to use a language successfully in real-life situations, they feel a sense of accomplishment and are more likely to continue using and learning the language, but remember to make it fun, impactful, and memorable...more about that soon.

I wish somebody would've told me that!

The following pie chart shows an example of what 25 hours of language exposure a week may look like for a family.

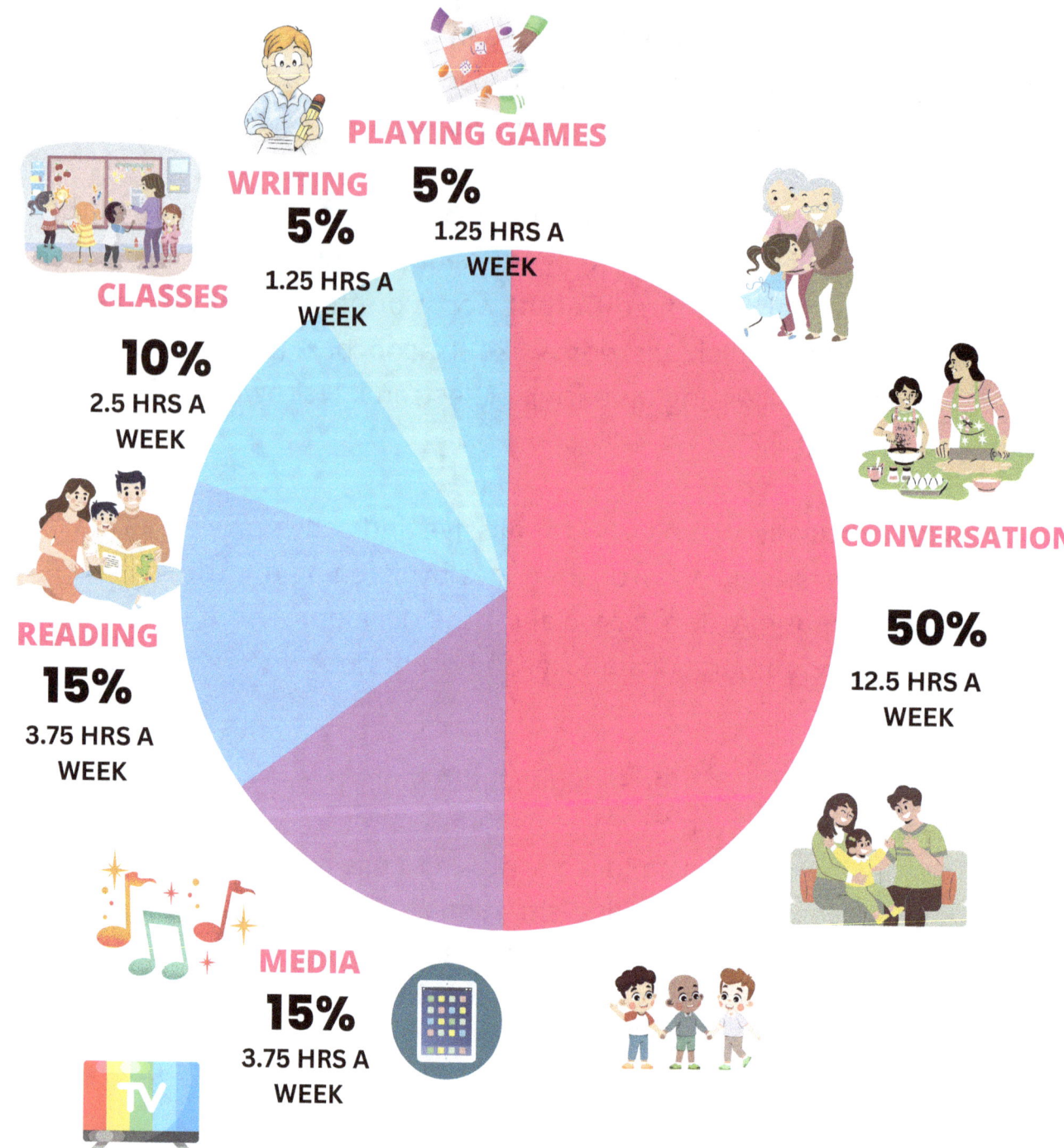

PLAYING GAMES
5%
1.25 HRS A WEEK

WRITING
5%
1.25 HRS A WEEK

CLASSES
10%
2.5 HRS A WEEK

READING
15%
3.75 HRS A WEEK

MEDIA
15%
3.75 HRS A WEEK

CONVERSATION
50%
12.5 HRS A WEEK

25 HOURS OF LANGUAGE EXPOSURE

Nobody told me...

The Importance of Creating a Positive Emotional Connection to the Language for My Child.

I was raised in a house where the motto, "En esta casa solo se habla Español," (We only speak Spanish in this house) was used. For many years, I resented my parents for forcing me to speak Spanish, especially when I wanted to express myself in other ways.

You may say I rebelled quite a bit, and when my parents decided to move us from the US to Colombia at the age of 13, well, let's just say I gave my parents more than they bargained for.

Even though I initially hated my parents for having us move to my birth country, which I had very few memories of, as I grew up, I realized how powerful an emotional connection I had with it and, thus, the language.

It created memories of being around my extended family, laughing, and playing games. It brought folklore and legends alive.

I experienced some of the most memorable experiences in Spanish like my first concert, my first hike in the mountains, my first neighborhood Christmas fiesta, my first boyfriend, you get the idea.

The emotional connection is so strong that I can tell you that I pray and curse in Spanish, lol.

When I started raising my daughter bilingually, I knew that I didn't want her to resent the language or me. I didn't want to create a forceful environment, but I did want to create an intentional one.

That meant being understanding if my daughter couldn't express herself in one language and preferred the other. That meant practicing a lot of patience and doubting myself whether she was learning enough. Most importantly, I wanted to make sure that she was having strong positive emotional connections to the language so she could view the language as a positive force in her life.

How have I helped her create a strong positive connection to the language when she is not immersed in the language or culture as I was, when she lives away from her extended family, and when we are also incorporating a 3rd language?

Focus on **MAKING IT FUN, making it impactful, and making memories.**

I wish somebody would've told me that!

How To Make the Minority Language Fun, Impactful, & Memorable

These are a few ways you can create a positive connection to the language.

1

Create a "1st" Experience

Think of fun ways you can incorporate the minority language into their first experiences, like a first concert, first family trip, first playdate, or even naming your first pet in the minority language.

2

Focus on Bonding

When you focus on creating a bond first in the minority language, it takes the language from being merely a subject to a point of connection between you and your child. Talking, asking questions, laughing, showing empathy, and praising are all ways you can bond in the minority language.

3

Incorporate what they love

Find ways to incorporate what they love in the minority language. Do they love cooking shows? How about watching the cooking show in the minority language and making a recipe? Do they love music? How about playing some music in the minority language? Get creative and take cues from your child.

4

Incorporate people

Whenever possible, incorporate the language with people, so there is interaction. How about grandparents, having playdates, visiting with the extended family, visiting a restaurant, or cultural events?

5

Make it a tradition

Give them something to look forward to doing every year in the minority language. Maybe it's part of a holiday tradition, something you do on their birthday, or a special gift. When it's done with love, it'll be memorable.

50 Language Activities

To Encourage Language Development in Children 2 - 6 Years

1. Read books in both languages
2. Watch TV shows or movies in both languages
3. Play language-learning games
4. Have conversations in both languages
5. Listen to music in both languages
6. Cook together using recipes in both languages
7. Visit cultural events in both languages
8. Attend language classes together
9. Play memory games with words in both languages
10. Use flashcards to practice vocabulary in both languages
11. Sing songs in both languages
12. Play word games like Scrabble or Boggle in both languages
13. Go on a language-learning scavenger hunt
14. Tell stories in both languages
15. Write letters or emails to family members in both languages
16. Play charades using words in both languages
17. Play 'I Spy' in both languages
18. Go on a language-learning field trip to a museum or cultural center
19. Travel to your heritage country
20. Play language-learning board games
21. Practice language skills during everyday activities, like grocery shopping or running errands
22. Use bilingual storybooks to teach both languages simultaneously
23. Play "Simon Says" in both languages
24. Take turns reading paragraphs or pages from a book in both languages
25. Have a language-learning playdate with other bilingual families.

For Parents

26. Play language-learning video games
27. Make a language-learning journal and write in both languages
28. Listen to Spanish storytime podcasts
29. Listen to audiobooks in both languages
30. Use language-learning apps
31. Have a language-learning "show and tell"
32. Make a bilingual calendar and practice days of the week and months of the year in both languages
33. Go on a nature walk and label plants and animals in both languages
34. Practice counting in both languages
35. Play language-learning bingo
36. Make a language-learning memory book
37. Watch a TV show in one language with subtitles in the other language
38. Play Pictionary using words in both languages
39. Attend language immersion camps or programs
40. Use a bilingual dictionary to look up words
41. Play language-learning "20 questions"
42. Go to a bilingual story time at a library
43. Write stories in both languages
44. Make a bilingual family photo album and label pictures in both languages
45. Practice telling time in both languages
46. Play a language-learning version of "I Spy" with colors and shapes
47. Practice saying tongue twisters in both languages
48. Make a bilingual map of your town or city and label landmarks in both languages
49. Practice grammar and sentence structure in both languages
50. Cook your favorite traditional dish in both languages.

Remember, the key to bilingual learning is consistency and repetition. Keep practicing and using both languages in everyday activities, and your child will become a confident and fluent bilingual speaker!

Nobody told me...

Consistently Speaking Spanish (or the Minority Language) May Be Hard.

Remember, I grew up with the MLAH method where only Spanish was spoken at the home. Since my parents didn't "teach" us Spanish, I figured it would be a similar experience with my daughter.

Boy, was I wrong. Spanish was my first language, but because English speakers surrounded my environment as an adult, including my husband, my comfort level with Spanish decreased while my comfort level in English increased.

I got so used to speaking English all the time, except with my family and some friends, that switching to just Spanish seemed very awkward. I can tell you that I never just spoke Spanish to my daughter. I tried, but nope, it was hard.

Your case may be totally different, and it's terrific if you can maintain a high level of minority language exposure, but in other cases, that may not be realistic.

I wish somebody would've told me that!

How To Feel More Comfortable Speaking the Minority Language

There are a few key things that you can do to help you build confidence in the minority language.

1

Immerse Yourself in the Language

Try to surround yourself with the language as much as possible. This can include watching movies or TV shows in the minority language,

2

Practice consistently

Practice speaking the minority language as much as possible. Even if you make mistakes or stumble over your words, keep practicing. The more you practice, the more comfortable you will become.

3

Find a language partner

Find someone who speaks the minority language and practice speaking with them regularly. This can be a friend or a language exchange partner. Speaking with someone else can help build your confidence and improve your fluency.

4

Take a language course

Consider taking a language course to improve your grammar, vocabulary, and pronunciation. This can help you become more comfortable speaking the minority language.

5

Set achievable goals

Set achievable goals for yourself and track your progress. This can help you stay motivated and focused on your language learning journey.

"Bilingual parenting isn't easy but someone has to do it in order for us to stay connected and understand our cultures and heritage."

—Christine "Tacos" Blandino
Bilingual Parenting Mom & STEM Educator
Lego®Masters Contestant

Nobody told me...

Trust Your Instincts Even If It Goes Against the Experts

When you have a baby and walk out of the hospital, you don't walk out with a manual that reads, "How to raise a child." Although, I'm sure you wish you did.

Yes, of course, you do lots of reading, watch lots of YouTube videos, Google everything, and ask your friends and family questions; quick to learn that EVERYONE will have an opinion about everything when it comes to raising a child. Why? Because everyone has done it perfectly. Ok, just kidding, but they think they have. Am I wrong?

Of course, they mean well, but what happens is that the moment you have your baby, you start to second guess yourself because, well, you aren't an expert. You're a new mommy or daddy, right?

You revert to the books, videos, and message friends to help you figure it out, whatever the "it" happens to be.

But many times, you neglect your instincts.

When I started this bilingual parenting journey, I didn't know what I was doing right or wrong.

Instinctively, I knew that I had to continue. Instinctively, I knew that if I kept talking to my daughter in Spanish, she would learn also. However, because I kept comparing and listening to "this method is the best method," I thought my daughter wasn't learning Spanish.

I became frustrated and impatient when I didn't hear my daughter reciprocate.

I wanted my daughter to respond in beautiful and eloquent Spanish sentences, but instead, she ended up with a lot of Spanglish (which is ok, by the way, and a sign that they ARE learning).

It took a long while to understand that my daughter WAS learning Spanish even when I thought she wasn't.
It also taught me what most bilingual parenting books and experts don't teach: to trust your instincts.

I once interviewed a mom on my podcast, The Latina Mom Legacy, who shared that her son had experienced a speech delay.
Her child's doctors recommended that her son see an English-speaking speech & language pathologist. They also recommended that she speak to her son in English and stop speaking Spanish.

Instinctively, she knew she did not want to stop speaking to her son in Spanish. Instinctively, she knew she had to find a Spanish-speaking SLP, so she did.

After months of therapy, going against the experts, and trusting her instincts, her son was able to not only overcome his speech delay but become fully bilingual AND gifted.

While you may not be an expert at languages or even bilingual parenting right now, you will become the expert at knowing YOUR child, and that is something nobody can teach you.

Learn to trust your instincts.

I wish somebody would've told me that!

"The intuitive mind is a sacred gift, and the rational mind is a faithful servant. We have created a society that honors the servant and has forgotten the gift."

—Albert Einstein

Nobody told me...

It Will Be a Roller Coaster Ride.

Because my parents made it look so straightforward, I didn't expect this journey to have so many turns or highs and lows.

Don't get me wrong, I love a good roller coaster, but this roller coaster ride is long!

I have watched my daughter dance to Spanish songs as a baby, love Spanish as a toddler, completely hate it when she started school, sing her heart out in Spanish at her very first concert (gracias Marc Anthony), read Spanish books cover to end only to later hate it.

Does that sound like a roller coaster or what?!

You will go through seasons of growth, regression, joy, and frustration. When you understand this, you can adapt or pivot if needed.

If something works for your child and you see language progress, great! Continue to do that.

If something isn't working out, you can change course and adapt quickly because it doesn't surprise you.

You can also express great joy as your child responds in Spanish or the minority language and you hear them say, "Quiero Leche." (I want milk.) Yes! Progress.

You may also experience frustration as you feel stuck, like your child doesn't "want to learn," or worse, think they "hate Spanish" or the minority language.

All those emotions come up, from highs to lows to seasons where it's simply constant. This is what a bilingual parenting journey MAY look like. Just to let you know, I didn't say that it's what it DOES look like.

That is because every family is different, and every experience is different. I share mine because these are things nobody ever told me I MAY experience raising a bilingual child.

You may not experience this, and raising a bilingual child for you and your family may be a piece of cake.

But just in case it's not, now you know!

I wish somebody would've told me that!

Write down 5 expectations that you have for your bilingual parenting journey.

1

2

3

4

5

Nobody told me...

As the Child Gets Older, It Will Be Easier and Yet More Challenging

Well, what does this mean?

When your child isn't able to verbalize yet, the challenge is knowing whether they are learning, but I already covered that in a previous chapter. However, there are many resources available... from books to bilingual storytime at the library to toys and so much more.

Until age 5, you have many resources to help you raise a bilingual child. This makes it easier for young children and you as you raise a bilingual child.

However, as your child gets older, while their level and acquisition of language may be good or even great and thus easier, MAINTAINING that level will become increasingly MORE DIFFICULT.

Why?

Well, there are many factors.

Your child starting school is probably the most common factor. Having been immersed with you or a Spanish (or minority language) caregiver and hearing the minority language a lot, this will change once they begin school. They may likely rebel and may want to speak something other than Spanish or the minority language.

You may also find yourself speaking more English (or the majority language) because you will find yourself helping them with their homework in the majority language. If you're lucky enough to have your child in an immersion program, balancing both languages may be 50/50. Either way, their daily exposure may reduce.

Another reason it becomes more complicated when they're older is that the resources and products that appeal to the older child in the majority language aren't typically available in Spanish (or the minority language). Companies are getting better at bilingual resources, but there are still limitations.

Yet another factor is that parents miss the point about making sure Spanish is FUN for kids. Kids need to associate Spanish with positive emotions but if they feel it is a drag or, worse, feel forced, they will resent the language or you for enforcing it.

I wish somebody would've told me that!

"The increasing demand for bilingualism proves the need for only more resources and more language immersion programs. How thrilling to know we're helping to cultivate a more culturally empathetic generation of children. Global citizens are our future!"

—Stephanie Moran Reed
Founder of Mija Books

How To Make Language Learning Fun For Older Kids

There are a few key things that you can do to help make language learning fun for older children.

1

Use technology
Encourage the use of language learning apps, videos, podcasts, and games that are designed for their age group. These tools make learning more interactive and engaging.

2

Tune in to your child and make it relevant
Choose topics that are interesting and relevant to your child's life, such as music, movies, or sports. If they like it in the majority language, they'll be open to it in the minority language. This can make learning more meaningful and enjoyable.

3

Focus on conversation
Practice speaking with your child or encourage them to practice speaking with friends or extended family members, even through video chat. This helps them to feel more confident and motivated to learn.

4

Make it social
Organize language learning activities or minority language playdates with other learners of the same age. This creates a social and fun atmosphere that can make learning more enjoyable.

5

Use humor
Incorporate humor and jokes into language learning. This can make learning more lighthearted and enjoyable

Nobody told me...

Having a Language Network Is Imperative

Can you raise a bilingual child on your own? Sure. Will it be easy? Well, that depends on you and how your child learns.

Here's the thing, it's much easier when you have an extended language network that you can rely on. What does that mean? It means having people in your life who will help you in your bilingual parenting journey.

Who are these people?

Everyone from abuela and abuelo (the grandparents), your extended family close or far away, your child's minority language-speaking teacher, your friends, the minority language-speaking parents at school or daycare, the librarian at bilingual storytime, even your Spanish, Italian, or Chinese-speaking waiter at your local restaurant.

These are all people that can assist and complement your bilingual parenting, whether they know it or not.

It's essential to grow your Spanish (or minority language) network because the more exposure your child has to the minority language and the more opportunities you can present to them to listen, speak, and use it, the stronger their language muscle becomes.

That's right. Language is like toning your arms or bicep muscles; the more you work on it, the more developed it becomes. That being said, much like growing your biceps, bicep curls alone may not be enough to get you that definition you're looking for, so you may resort to pushups, dips, or perhaps take up a sport like tennis or basketball to change the range of motion your arm is getting to enhance those muscles further.

Language can be treated similarly, and so having a diverse minority language network with people that sound differently, have different accents, say things differently than you do at home, or have different ethnic backgrounds can help your child and even strengthen those language muscles.

My Family's Bilingualism Support Network

These are our extended family, friends, or people in our community that speak the minority language and can support us:

NAME	RAISING BILINGUAL	LIVES NEARBY
01	☐	☐
02	☐	☐
03	☐	☐
04	☐	☐
05	☐	☐
06	☐	☐
07	☐	☐
08	☐	☐
09	☐	☐
10	☐	☐
11	☐	☐
12	☐	☐

How To Get Support From Your Bilingualism Support Network

There are a few key things that you can do to help you get more support throughout your bilingual parenting journey:

1

Communicate your needs

Be clear about the kind of support you seek from your bilingual parenting network. Are you looking for resources on language learning, tips on maintaining a bilingual home, or simply emotional support?

2

Attend events or host one

Attend events and activities organized by your bilingual parenting network or host one yourself. This can be a great way to connect with other bilingual families, share ideas and experiences, and build a support system.

3

Participate in online groups or forums

There are many bilingual and multilingual parenting groups online where members share ideas and advice. Participate in these forums, ask questions, and contribute your own experiences. Check out my resources page to see how you can join my FB group.

4

Connect one-on-one with friends & family

Reach out to friends and family members and include them in your bilingual parenting. Let them know why this matters to you and how they can help and support you in this journey. Be open-minded; they are helping.

5

Be open and honest

Be open and honest about your experiences and struggles with raising bilingual children. This can create a safe and supportive environment where everyone feels comfortable sharing their own challenges and successes.

Nobody told me...

You Will Want to Give Up Many Times.

Or this journey will be super easy, and I hope that's the case for you! Listen, as I keep mentioning, every family's experience is different. In my family, we've wanted to give up several times, both my husband raising our daughter to speak Bulgarian and I raising our daughter to speak Spanish.

Why would you want to give up? Well, sometimes life happens, and other things become a priority. Remember when I told you that you go through seasons? Yes, there may be seasons when you'll want to quit.

My dad passed away in 2020 from Covid. When the world had shut down, and my daughter had just a few weeks of starting Kindergarten virtually, I lost my hero.

For the next few months, I found myself an emotional wreck, traveling and taking care of my now-widowed mom while my husband took over parenting duties back home.

Was language learning a priority for me? Nope. Was it a priority for my family? Nope.

Did I want to quit? Yes and no, but months later, when I started to feel like myself again, I continued being more consistent with Spanish.

My husband, too, finds himself frustrated and wants to throw in the towel occasionally, but we go back to our why. The root of why we want to raise a bilingual daughter and pivot, perhaps change strategy if we need to and continue, but we continue.

If you expect to raise a fluent child, this is a long journey, but it's very rewarding. You may have times when you'll want to quit, or perhaps you see that your child isn't learning ANY language, and you're afraid that by teaching your child two or even three languages, it's your fault they are showing signs of regression or delay.

You're human to be scared and to question things. I can tell you that researchers believe bilingualism is not to be blamed for a child's speech delay, so instead of quitting when you become scared, get informed, and yes, seek the help that you need.

It's normal to want to give up, and it's normal to want to give up many times. It may not be easy, but you can succeed if you keep going.

"*A new generation of Latina moms is embracing our ancestry and roots with pride. As we embrace the greatness of who we are as a culture, and all we can contribute to the US and its future, we know that our Spanish language is a valuable asset versus a source of shame. Our legacy is to equip our kids with the ability to be bilingual, which increases not just their opportunities as they step into the world, but it also elevates the prospects of this country we call home.*"

—Valeria Aloe
Author, Entrepreneur,
and Founder of the Rising Together movement

How To Stay Motivated in Your Bilingual Parenting Journey

There are a few key things that you can do to stay motivated in this bilingual parenting journey:

1

Start with your why

Understanding why you want to raise a bilingual child will help keep you going when the journey gets difficult. Seeing the long-term goal will help you stay motivated to keep going.

2

Set realistic goals

Learning a language takes time, and it's important to set realistic goals for both you and your child. Start with small, achievable goals and celebrate your successes along the way. Remember, take it one step at a time.

3

Consistency is key

Consistency is crucial when it comes to language learning. Try to establish a routine that incorporates language learning into your daily life, such as reading a book in the second language before bedtime. Oh, and write it down and schedule it.

4

Connect with other bilingual families

Joining a community of other bilingual families can provide support and motivation for you and your child. It will also make you feel understood and may help answer questions you have along your journey.

5

Be patient and persistent. Give Yourself Grace!

Learning a language is a journey, and there will be ups and downs along the way. Be patient with yourself and your child, and keep pushing forward. Don't give up!

Nobody told me...

It Is Very Lonely at Times and You'll Learn to Be "Unpopular"

You may think, "well, that's a bit dramatic!" but hear me out.

If you live in the United States (or any majority English-speaking country) and want to raise a bilingual child, you're a minority. Unfortunately, only a slight emphasis is placed in American culture or in our school systems on the benefits of being bilingual as a society. According to a 2018 study by Pew Research, "Throughout all 50 states and the District of Columbia, 20% of K-12 students are enrolled in foreign language classes, according to a 2017 report from the nonprofit American Councils for International Education."

Compare that with "a median of 92% of European students are learning a language in school."

A European Union survey showed that as much as 58% of the European population speak two languages, compared to just 22% in the US.

So if you live in the United States and you live outside a diverse metropolitan area, you may also experience language racism, especially when it comes to Spanish or other non-Anglo languages.

On top of that, your extended family may live far away, and your Spanish network (or minority language network) may be non-existent.

The minority language may also be YOUR first language, your mother tongue, and your first memories may have been built around the minority language. Perhaps for you, it's not just about the language; it's about your identity, heritage, and family values. The thought of losing that when it feels like it's only your responsibility IS lonely.

I hear you and assure you that you're not alone.

Yes, you may be the only one/s in your circle of parent friends (including minority language-speaking ones) to be raising bilingual children, and you may even risk losing some of those friends.

Yes, you may encounter dirty looks as you speak to your child in Español (or the minority language) in public.

Yes, you may not have the resources that other more populated areas have...

But I know you are gifting your child a more valuable gift than you know, a gift they will use and benefit from well into their old age, even after you're gone.

However, If being popular is important to you, this journey may not be for you, and I'm telling you that in the sincerest of ways.

As Albert Einstein once said,

"What is right is not always popular, and what is popular is not always right."

Now you must determine what you feel is right for your family and be prepared mentally so that you and your family aren't like everyone else.

That, my friend, is NOT a bad thing!

I wish somebody would've told me that!

Why did you pick up this book? Sit down for a moment and write down why you want to raise a bilingual child.

Nobody told me...

This Is Actually an Amazing Gift With More Benefits Than You Realize.

I'm sure you've heard that raising a bilingual child is good, but do you know precisely why? You would know only if you like doing a ton of research (like me) before you dive into something.

Now let me tell you that deciding to raise your child bilingually is probably one of the best gifts you can give your child...definitely way better than anything on Amazon!

Why is raising a bilingual child so beneficial?

Let's start with studies showing that bilingual people tend to have better cognitive brain function than monolinguals.

According to a research study performed by Bialystok, Kausanskaya & Marian, children who had five to ten years of bilingual exposure had averaged higher scores in cognitive performance, greater attention, focus distraction resistance, decision-making, judgment, and responsiveness to feedback.

The MRI scans of these children revealed greater activity in the prefrontal cortex networks directing these and other executive functions.

Can you say smarter? No, really.

I can tell you from my experience that I have seen my daughter thrive in school, going from 1st to 2nd grade in months. She has also developed quick reflex skills in hockey. If you ask me, I attribute her academic and athletic growth to being raised trilingually.

Research also suggests that bilinguals adapt quickly to their environments, and children and adolescents who speak more than one language may reach adulthood with better brain structure. Bilingualism may also delay the onset of Alzheimer's and dementia.

Bilinguals tend to be more empathetic towards people different than them as they are exposed to different cultures and perhaps people that sound differently, thus developing a deeper understanding of a larger world.

On top of all that, the average bilingual earns about 5-20% more than monolinguals. Can you say cha-ching?

Do you need more evidence? If you do a quick search on the internet for "benefits of bilingualism," you will see tons of articles and medical journal reports on all sorts of studies. This is fascinating and worth the reading time. However, if you don't have the time or don't need the additional information, at least you have a more informed picture after reading this.

I sort of knew that being bilingual does something to your brain in a good way and that "people" said it was a good thing, but beyond that, I had no idea how truly impactful it was.

More importantly, I didn't know there were so many side benefits that would positively impact my daughter's life in so many ways. Because I did the extra reading early on, I knew that not raising her bilingually would be a total disservice to her.

However, if I had not known...

I wish somebody would've told me that!

Benefits of Bilingualism

1   **Improved cognitive abilities**
Research has shown that bilingualism can improve cognitive abilities like memory, attention, and problem-solving skills. Bilingual individuals also tend to perform better on standardized tests.

2   **Improved communication skills**
Bilingual individuals have a better understanding of language structure and usage, which can improve their communication skills in both their first and second languages.

3   **Improved academic performance**
Bilingual students often perform better academically, particularly in areas such as reading, writing, and math.

4   **Improved athletic performance**
Because of the improved cognitive abilities, many bilingual athletes show fast reflexes, quicker decision-making skills, and mental stamina.

5   **Enhanced cultural awareness**
Knowing a second language can help you gain a deeper understanding and appreciation of other cultures, leading to increased empathy and tolerance.

6   **Increased job opportunities**
Being bilingual can make you more marketable in the job market, particularly in industries that require interaction with people who speak different languages.

Where Do You Go From Here?

If you're feeling a bit overwhelmed by all the information in this book, that's quite understandable. Raising a bilingual child can feel like an arduous task. Believe me, I know exactly how you feel.

As long as you understand your expectations for yourself and your family, you'll be well on your way. Remember, this is a long journey and not one that happens overnight, but the value that you will be adding to your child's life is priceless, even if it doesn't feel so at times.

If, after reading this book, I have scared you away from raising a bilingual child, then please take my sincerest apologies, and I beg you to reconsider. Yes, it may not be easy, but it's not impossible!

On the following page, you will have a bilingual parenting checklist. This will help you ensure you're on the path to success in your bilingual journey.

Bilingual Parenting Checklist

✔	The Basics Checklist	Notes
	I know where I want to go in this bilingualism journey and what level of proficiency I want my child to have.	
	I've had "THE LANGUAGE TALK" with my spouse or significant other.	
	I know who will speak to my child in what language, how often, and when.	
	I have written down all the people in my minority language network that can support me in this bilingual parenting journey.	
	I have written down what my expectations are for this journey.	
	I have written down WHY I want to raise a bilingual child.	
	I have created a budget for my child's language learning.	

Conclusion

I hope you found this book helpful in your bilingual parenting journey.

Remember, you are not alone, and YOU CAN raise a bilingual child!

In the following few pages, you will find links to resources to help you continue your bilingual parenting journey. You will also find details for my on-demand online course, How to Raise a Bilingual Spanish Child Practically, which was created, much like this book, from an educated parent's perspective but with practical applications for parents wanting to raise bilinguals.

Some Helpful Resources

Mi Legasi Blogs

The Mi Legasi Blogs are a great place to find links to my favorite bilingual Spanish books about Hispanic heritage and Bilingual Parenting.

https://www.milegasi.com/pages/blogs

The Latina Mom Legacy Podcast

A podcast for Latina Moms or multicultural families who want to create a Spanish language and Hispanic heritage legacy for their children. Join me as I interview Latina moms, language and heritage experts, and community change-makers to motivate you to stay on your bilingual parenting journey.

https://thelatinamomlegacy.com

Mi Legasi Bilingual Printables

Check out some printables you can use with your child at home.

https://www.milegasi.com/collections/printables-shop

Become an Online Student and Learn How to Raise a Bilingual Spanish Child Your Way

Raising a bilingual child is possible and a gift so valuable for your child's future. I created this course to answer all your questions because, like you, when I started this bilingual parenting journey, it wasn't clear to me.

I want to save you time and headaches and empower you with the tools you will need to raise a bilingual child YOUR WAY...using your family's strengths and not focusing on your shortcomings.

Many bilingual parenting books and educators talk about the scientific stuff, and while that's great, few provide that in-the-trenches perspective that I bring, all in the comfort of your home. What do you say?

YES! I WANT TO ENROLL TODAY

https://milegasi.thinkific.com

What Parents & Specialists are Saying

BEST GIFT YOU WILL EVER GIVE YOUR CHILDREN
"This course is incredible!! Janny walks you through teaching your child Spanish...it doesn't matter where you are in your journey or how fluent you are...this course has you covered. Easy to follow. Best of all, it's taught from a place of authenticity and true experience! **This isn't just a course...this is an investment in your children's future!** ¡Cómpralo ya!"
—Astrid G. (parent)

"I honestly did not know what to expect and In my opinion
I am in AWWWWWE it went far and above. Well done." —Z.Z (parent)

EXCELLENT!
"This course is enjoyable and informative. **It's easy to follow at your own pace, and does a great job of explaining concepts in bilingual education for young children.**"
—S. Haren (Translator, Linguist)

"**As an SLP I really enjoyed this course.** The instructor made the process of learning personal and fun. She included videos and photos of her family to show her journey. Great course. **I would certainly recommend this to anyone who is interested in raising a Bilingual child.**"
—J. Curry (Speech Language Pathologist)

"**I've never taken any courses on how to raise bilingual children and I can honestly say after taking this course alone...there really is no need to take any other course.**"
—Melissa M. (parent)

"It's exciting to have a resource like Janny's course to aid in my children's bilingual journey. **The course definitely gave me a boost in confidence and reassured me that I can raise bilingual children.**"
—Jennifer Rojas

YES! I WANT TO ENROLL TODAY

https://milegasi.thinkific.com

Let's Connect

Instagram @milegasi

Follow for bilingual parenting tips and what's going on in the Mi Legasi community. Be sure to tag me with a picture of your book to share with our community!

Sign Up for The Newsletter at www.Milegasi.com

Get even more tips delivered to your inbox. Stay up to date with the latest blogs, podcast episodes, events, courses, and shop.

Join our Facebook Group

Mi Legasi - Bilingual Spanish Parenting Support Group

Do you have questions about YOUR situation?Join our private group to connect and engage with other parents wanting to raise bilingües. I am happy to answer your questions.

ABOUT THE AUTHOR

Janny Perez is a multilingual parenting mom, host of The Latina Mom Legacy podcast and a bilingual parenting educator who has created Mi Legasi (milegasi.com), an online platform with resources, blogs, courses and workshops, and shop for parents wanting to raise bilingual Spanish kids connected to their roots.

She is known for her Top 100 Apple Podcast in Parenting and Top 50 Global Podcast, The Latina Mom Legacy, which has been featured in New York Family Magazine, Hip Latina, and Fierce by Mitu for its influence on Latina moms, culture, and language. She has interviewed dozens of moms, language specialists, authors, and community change makers, all raising or influencing bilingual children. She has over 20 years of experience in design and education and has been podcasting since 2019.

Janny Perez's *Nobody Told Me THIS About Raising a Bilingual Child* is an easy and practical book for parents or parents-to-be full of bilingual parenting information often overlooked in other books. She was inspired to write a visual book with exercises and tips to help parents who may feel overwhelmed or intimidated by the subject of raising a bilingual child, much like she was at the beginning of her bilingual parenting journey. *Nobody Told Me THIS About Raising a Bilingual Child* has received rave reviews from parents, teachers, specialists, and authors. She is thrilled to share her experience with readers.

When Janny Perez isn't writing, podcasting, or working, she can be found taking a Zumba® or Yoga class, going on long nature walks with her dog, cheering her hockey goalie daughter at a game, or reading a book while sipping on her "cafecito."

Born in Medellín, Colombia, raised in Hialeah, FL, and educated in London, Chicago, and New York City, she now lives in New Jersey, USA, with her husband, 8-year-old daughter, and beagle retriever named Hope.

Janny Perez is positive and inspiring in her approach to bilingual parenting. She hopes that *Nobody Told Me THIS about Raising a Bilingual Child* will inspire and help readers raise bilingual children. She is excited about continuing to support parents in their bilingual parenting journey and reaching 1 million podcast downloads...in her words, "One cafecito at a time!"

FULL REVIEWS

"An Honest, Revealing, & Practical Book About Raising a Bilingual Child."

"An amazing and resourceful book about raising bilingual children that includes exercises for parents like creating a language plan and activity ideas that parents can use to engage with their children. Most importantly, raising a bilingual child is not easy but with consistency and tools like this book it can be possible."
— Dasy Perez, Expert Early Childhood Educator

"This book is a call to action. I've never been so encouraged to pursue this journey."
— Christine "Tacos" Blandino, STEM Educator

"In this insightful and revealing book, filled with practical guidance and beautiful illustrations, Janny Perez brings to the forefront her extensive wisdom around the challenges, resistance and self-doubt that arise when raising bilingual children. Most importantly, she offers effective and easy-to-apply ideas to support your journey as you create a meaningful legacy for your loved ones."
— Valeria Aloe. Author, Entrepreneur, and Founder of the Rising Together movement